MW01278627

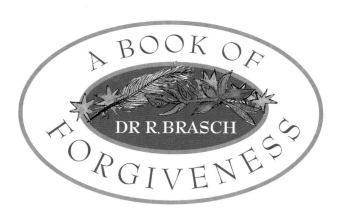

A BOOK OF

FORGIVENESS

DR R. BRASCH

Angus&Robertson
An imprint of HarperCollins*Publishers*

For Stephen and Wendy Baer,
friends one can always count on.

ACKNOWLEDGEMENTS

As in all my writing and work, Li, my wife, has been a
constant participant from the earliest stages of the preparation
of the manuscript and then beyond it, to the final proofreading.
Words cannot express my gratitude.

My thanks go out to Father J.V. Glynn of the Marist Fathers
for all the information he gave me about his late brother
Father Tony Glynn, and to the Reverend Terry Sweetser of the
First Universalist Church, Minneapolis, MN, USA,
for permitting me to quote part of his sermon
'Saying Yes to Yourself'.

I am also indebted to Professor A.H. Johns of the
Australian National University, Professor M.A. Soofi
and the Reverend D. Webster for all their
kind help. I wish to express my appreciation as well to
Marjan Karimpour and the Baha'i Information Centre,
Graeme Lyall and the Buddhist Council of NSW,
Mr T. O'Loghlan, Brother Emmanuel
and the Catholic Enquiry Centre, and Shelagh Garland
and the Religious Society of Friends.

Greatly appreciated was the assistance given to me by the
librarians of the Australian Broadcasting Corporation,
the Catholic Press Newspaper Co.,
Moore Theological College, the State Library of NSW
and the Woollahra Public Library.

Scripture quotations are from *The New King James Version*,
copyright © 1982 by Thomas Nelson Inc. Used by permission.

Quotation from *Love is the Answer* by G. Jampolsky copyright © 1990
by Bantam Books, a divison of Doubleday Dell Publishing.
Use by permission.

I would also like to thank the Estate of Robert Louis Stevenson
and Chatto and Windus for giving me permission to
quote from his writings and prayers.

Every effort has been made to contact the copyright
owners of the material in this book. Where this has not
been possible, the Publishers invite the persons
concerned to contact them.

Contents

FOREWORD

E ACH ONE OF US, at one time or another,
needs to forgive or to be forgiven.
Wrongs done, injustices suffered and conflicts that
divide, unless rectified and resolved,
will haunt and hurt us.
This hurt may be so deep that it will
dangerously affect, if not poison, our lives. Feelings
of hatred and bitterness can
imprison us in the past, perhaps even leading
to obsessive behaviour. We could end up
living under constant stress, a factor which is now
known to be detrimental to
both our attitude to life and our health.

No legislation or private or public shaking
of hands can be of lasting consequence, unless the
victim and the offender have together reached
reconciliation. This is why forgiveness is of such
paramount importance in our time, a time which is so
full of the many rifts that can occur in human
relationships, such as the breaking up of families
and interracial strife.
To receive and to give forgiveness is not always
easy. It may prove an arduous process, but it can be
done. To help you in your pursuit of forgiveness (or
perhaps for those whom you may wish to help), I have
written this book. It discusses the need for forgiveness

and suggests a variety of practical steps to guide you on
your way, as well as providing insight into how to
choose the right moment to embark upon your effort.
Simultaneously, this book points to the dangers
and problems you may encounter in your quest, such as
the rejection of an apology. It offers suggestions as to
how to face and overcome these problems. There is also
a charming story illustrating how to teach our young
the importance and practice of forgiveness.

This book deals with such questions as to whether
a benevolent God can be blamed (or should be forgiven)
for so much innocent suffering in the world,
and whether we can ever forget, even if we forgive,
the wrongs done to us.

Further added to these 'whys', 'whens' and 'hows' is
a selection of stories, anecdotes and examples, showing
the pursuit and result of forgiveness throughout the
world and through the centuries. Quotations,
interspersed between the various topics, may also inspire
you. I hope that you will find this book of much
use and benefit.

R.B.

Words Tell — The Semantics of Forgiveness

WORDS CAN SAY much when one investigates their roots. Words do so, not least, in the arena of forgiveness, clarifying some of its concepts and stressing specific aspects of its practice. The term 'forgiveness' is a combination of 'for' and 'to give'. The prefix 'for' intensifies the meaning of what is to follow. Those who forgive, therefore, do not merely 'give' in the ordinary sense of the word, but do so with a special intensity — ardently they lavish a gift on those who have done wrong to them.

Significantly, the alternative use of the word 'pardon' — often applied in a more legal sense — has the same essential meaning. 'Par' (from the Latin *per*) is yet another prefix that is meant to intensify the concept that it precedes. The ending 'don' is a shortening of the Latin *donare*, also meaning 'to give', which is reflected in the term 'donation'. Hence, to 'pardon' reiterates the fact that forgiveness is a special 'gift'.

Those who experience conflict are said to have 'fallen out' when they separate themselves from each other, just as sinners, in religious tradition, distance themselves from God. In either case, the person concerned is no

longer at ease. By gaining forgiveness however, we become again 'at one' with our fellow humans, with society and, religiously speaking, with God. We make ourselves 'whole'. This closing of the gap, this reunion and becoming 'at one', has created the term 'at-one-ment', or atonement.

Reconciliation, the final aim of all forgiveness, etymologically speaks of 'coming together again', a restoring of former relationships. Amnesty, particularly used in cases of a government or court granting a pardon to offenders, is of Greek origin. Like the concept of amnesia, it refers to 'not remembering', that is, 'forgetting' the offence that has been committed. All these words explain the meaning behind the simple terms we use to describe the phenomenon of forgiveness.

THE NEED FOR FORGIVENESS

Forgiving and Forgetting

FORGIVING AND FORGETTING play a significant role in the arena of human relationships. However, they are not as simple as they might at first appear. Some hurts may indeed be so insignificant that they are not even worth taking note of, far less remembering. Many are the instances in which when an apology is made, it is rejected as unnecessary, the forgiver generally saying, 'Oh, forget it!'.

Not less common, but more ungracious, is a forgiver's assurance that 'I shall forgive, but I shall not forget'. In fact, the second part of this 'promise' weakens, if not almost undoes, the good of the first. It reflects an emotional attitude of retained animosity and shows that the conflict is not totally resolved. It might even contain an implied threat or challenge. It makes forgiveness unreal and incomplete, and the two parties cannot thus attain a genuine reconciliation.

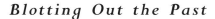

Blotting Out the Past

'I SHALL FORGIVE, but I shall not forget.' This statement's wording undoes any good intentions or results. Nevertheless, objectively considered, there is still the question of whether it is ever possible to forget. Can we really blot out the past? It can be assumed that however hard we try, we cannot necessarily wipe out a memory, especially if it is emotionally charged. There may well be a part of the brain which permanently stores traumatic experiences. We may not be able, therefore, to eliminate these experiences from our memory. These memories may continue, if only unconsciously, to haunt us for the rest of our lives. This is perhaps the greatest difficulty to be met in the practice of forgiveness.

Some cases present a further and more perturbing problem. Even if it were possible, should we forget? In doing so, we may be desecrating the memory of someone near and dear: the victim of the offence. Obvious examples of this problem relate to the holocaust and the many other brutalities committed in almost every part of the world, at one time or another, in the pursuit of racial, tribal, religious or ethnic predominance. Should any one of the survivors try to forget the atrocities committed to a parent, brother, sister or child? Would a genuine attempt to dismiss such a memory from the mind demonstrate disloyalty and thereby create a sense of guilt?

We need to heal the pain left by the past, but not necessarily forget that the past ever happened. This is the purpose of the many types of monuments erected to honour victims, which may be in the form of statues and museums or 'living memorials', such as institutions to aid the sick, the underprivileged and vulnerable, or even those that assist in the conservation of the threatened natural world, such as the planting of forests. Significantly, however, their purpose is to show concern that the victims should not be forgotten, but not to perpetuate hatred.

Forgiving presupposes remembering.

(Paul Tillich)

Individual Considerations

THERE ARE ALWAYS two sides to a story, and the major merit of those who forgive is that it is their initiative to try to re-establish a relationship that has broken down. It is so easy to exaggerate a hurt and thereby, instead of healing a breach which in many a case is of a very trivial nature, make it all the wider.

Life is complex and so are the occasions when we might feel snubbed, slighted or harmed. However, the intensity of our feelings may not correspond with the gravity of the offence. We must learn to keep a proper sense of proportion. We might even wisely learn to ignore what really is too insignificant to take notice of. Frequently we remember the one incident that hurt us, but forget the numberless moments of happiness and joy experienced in the past. Common sense should make us realise that by forgiving the offender we take charge of the situation, whilst if we retain feelings of hurt, we give the wrongdoer the upper hand.

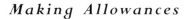

Making Allowances

PEOPLE DIFFER. Everyone has some weakness or failing.
Some individuals are endowed with an impetuous
nature. They are easily roused to anger which then
passes quickly like a thunderstorm. Others, of the
opposite disposition, will hide their feelings when
upset. Either behaviour is merely part of a person's
nature and must be taken into consideration when
a conflict occurs. Do not imagine that a person's
behaviour is specific to you. Instead it belongs to our
nature and we probably cannot do otherwise.
Accept people as they are and do not take personally
what was not really meant to harm you.

**No sin is too big for God to pardon, and none is
too small for habit to magnify.**

(Bachya)

A Matter of Acceptance

SOME PEOPLE ARE pliable and in a quarrel
or disagreement they are prepared to listen, and then
consider the other's point of view and side of the story.
With goodwill on the part of both, an eventual
reconciliation will occur. However if, perhaps through
factors beyond our control, the other party remains
inflexible and deaf to any argument, and it becomes
impossible to change the circumstances, we still must
not sever our relations. Instead, we should accept
realistically the situation, and in an understanding and
forgiving spirit adjust our attitude.

An adage reminds us:

For every evil under the sun
There is a remedy or there is none.
If there is one, try to find it,
If there isn't, never mind it!

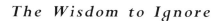

The Wisdom to Ignore

TO BE UNFORGIVING at times may say less about the
severity of the offence than about the lack
of understanding on the part of the offended. There
are many occasions when the ability to ignore
proves a significant asset, and replaces any necessity
for forgiveness.

Everyone makes blunders and, particularly in the heat
of the moment, says or does something which, though
inconsequential, can deeply hurt. There may not have
been a deliberate or evil motive or any intention to do
harm. Dispassionately looked upon, those slights
and bruises may have been merely the result
of thoughtlessness. Also, in an emotionally charged
atmosphere, we can become overly sensitive and take
personally what may have amounted to only a foolish,
though regrettable incident.

We lose nothing in dignity if we instantly dismiss from
our mind what has occurred. In fact, this will maintain,
if not enhance, our self-respect and keep a valuable
relationship intact.

Forgive what you can't excuse.
(Mary W. Montagu)

Bearing a Grudge

To BEAR A grudge for an injury suffered helps no-one. If anything, it is counterproductive. Instead of diminishing and eventually vanishing with time, the memory of the offence will weigh on you, growing ever heavier. Ultimately, you may be so obsessed by it that it will dominate your thinking and make a misery out of your life. A good example of this is the character of Miss Haversham in Charles Dickens' novel *Great Expectations*, who never disposed of her bridal gown after she was jilted on her wedding day. In fact, she continued to wear it, constantly recalling the shock she had suffered and thereby destroying her life. This behaviour did not necessarily demonstrate deep affection for the lover who cruelly abandoned her on the very day she had anticipated with such joy. Possibly, her action was prompted by self-pity. Unable to forgive him, she punished herself instead.

Never keep on bearing a grudge.

The things we remember best are those better forgotten.

(Baltasar Gracian)

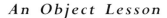

An Object Lesson

AN IMAGINATIVE headmaster had introduced at his school the annual holding of what he called a 'Grudge Day'. Always held in the autumn, it followed a fixed routine. On this day, the pupils were instructed to rake up all the dry leaves in the schoolgrounds and put them in a heap. Both pupils and teachers were then handed slips of paper on which to write any grudge they still nursed. The slips were collected and placed on top of the pile and, once everyone had gathered round, the headmaster set a match to the leaves and papers. As they went up in flames, all the grudges were regarded as having been symbolically consumed in the fire. Broken friendships were renewed, hurts and wrongs suffered were forgiven, and all felt the better for it.

It was a unique kind of lesson meant to foster in pupils and teachers alike a spirit of positive living. Mutually giving and receiving forgiveness destroys resentment and discontent. It leads to a realisation of the negativity of soured relationships and a recognition of the value of reconciliation. The tradition of a regularly recurring 'grudge day' prevented any harmful accumulation and perpetuation of grudges. Most of all, those participating in what was to become a ritual, experienced the exhilaration of forgiveness. 'What I gave, I have.'

Forgiveness is man's deepest need and highest achievement.

(Horace Bushnell)

16

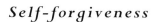

Self-forgiveness

HARDLY ANYONE goes through life being able to honestly
say that they have not erred at one time or another. We
may have left undone things we ought to have done
when there was still time. Unwittingly, we may have
postponed for too long expressing genuine love and
concern for those who not only merited it, but were
waiting for it, and to whom it would have given much
happiness. Our neglect may not have been due to the
fact that we did not care, but that we were 'too busy'.
Thus we put off for another day — which then never
came. We cannot make up for missed opportunities.

Another problem for self-reproach can be created early
in life when, immature and impetuous, we may have
given way to emotions and drives which in retrospect it
would have been wiser to keep under control. We
probably did not realise then the hurt they might cause
later on in life, not least to those we cherish most.

Do not start blaming yourself for past failings and
failures. This will only make your past spoil your future
and cause you to live in a continuous state of guilt.
Forgive yourself for what you are sorry to have done,
or for what you have irrevocably left undone
as a fallible human. Not releasing yourself from the
past would be unfair to you and to those
around you. In fact, by forgiving yourself you may
gain the strength to forgive others.

The wise man will make haste to forgive, because
he knows the true value of time, and will not
suffer it to pass away in unnecessary pain.

(Samuel Johnson)

TIMING
IS THE KEY

The Right Timing

HUMAN NATURE and circumstances widely differ. This makes the practice of forgiveness a complex and very personal process. There cannot be a general rule that encompasses everyone. We must thoughtfully choose the most appropriate way and the most propitious time to give or ask for forgiveness. Paradoxically, this may lead to contradictory advice with the choice dependent on each individual case. This especially applies to the right moment to seek or give forgiveness, and whether this time should be immediate or postponed, and if the latter, for how long. We simply cannot forgive on command.

It takes two sides to make a lasting peace, but it only takes one to make the first step.

(Edmund M. Kennedy)

Time Will Not Heal

IT IS A FALLACY to assume that a hurt will heal by itself. We might think that all we have to do is wait, as the passing of time leads the incident to become ever more remote, so that a relationship will automatically return to what it once was. However, to undo the harm demands careful and active attention.

To give your time and not your mind
Is like turning a mill with nothing to grind.

Reacting Rashly

AN INSULT MAY gravely upset us and, momentarily, make us impetuously do and say things which, after some quiet consideration, we would regard as unwise. Such a rash reaction will only aggravate the situation and make a future reconciliation very difficult indeed.

We must practice self-control even in the most trying of circumstances, and refrain from instantly 'hitting back'. Take time to consider your next move. Instead of trying to 'get even' and settle the score, give thought to how to deal rationally with the grievance and then open up ways that will lead to mutual forgiveness.

The wisest course for those who have been deeply hurt is to sleep on it. This was exactly the advice a man gave to his friend who, in his anger, expressed his determination of hitting back, quickly and strongly. 'Just regard the insult as mud,' the man suggested. Misinterpreting the remark, his friend said, 'That's just what it is — mud, and I'm going to clean it up!'. 'You should remember that mud can be brushed off much more easily when it is dry,' the man reminded him.

If we have to put down our foot, by all means let us do so. However, remember to step on the brake, and not the accelerator.

Many promising reconciliations have broken down because, while both parties came prepared to forgive, neither party came prepared to be forgiven.

(Charles Williams)

Let Things Cool Off a Little

THE TIME FOR giving and receiving forgiveness must be wisely chosen. Of course, to attempt to achieve forgiveness at once would be ideal, but in most instances this is impractical. If forgiveness is premature, it may spoil any future efforts. It is better to wait till the anger has subsided. Then, be on the alert for the opportunities that will offer themselves and seize them at once.

When a car's radiator is overheated, you will wisely not take off the cap until it has cooled down sufficiently. Ignoring such a precaution, the hot water would spurt out and possibly scald you. Yet we often make the mistake of dealing with people while we (and they) are still incensed and their minds, as it were, are 'overheated'. It is wiser to wait till everyone has cooled down. It is only then that you will be able to think and act clearly.

Albert Schweitzer, the renowned French clergyman, physician and Nobel Prize winner, was once asked what was wrong with people today. He replied that they simply did not think.

Lead us not into the temptation of believing that we have truly forgiven, while rancour lingers. . .
(Katherine Zell)

No Shortcut

You CANNOT EXPECT to instantly repair a breach that has occurred in a relationship. To achieve complete and lasting reconciliation you will have to work at it. It demands patience, takes time and may prove a slow process, possibly with many setbacks and the necessity of many new starts. Initial rebuffs should never discourage us from renewing our attempts.

Forgiveness is like the healing of a broken limb, which for some considerable time might need the support of splints for it to totally recover. Remember that it is well worth the effort for, with persistence, the moment will come when the splints are no longer necessary.

Very much taken by one of Sir Joshua Reynolds' paintings, a viewer expressed to the artist his admiration. 'That is a magnificent picture,' he said. 'It's not one picture,' Sir Joshua replied, 'it is ten pictures.' To produce it he had to paint and repaint it many times.

***I learnt that true forgiveness includes total
acceptance and out of acceptance wounds are
healed and happiness is possible again.***

(Catherine Marshall)

Don't Leave It
Till It Is Too Late

A FRIEND CALLED on his dying companion. For many years they had shared everything, even their innermost secrets. With death now imminent, they discussed a life that had been rich in experience. So that the dying man should pass away serenely, in peace of mind, his friend asked him whether there was anything he had done during his eventful life which worried him.

'I've no regrets for the things I've done,' the man replied. 'But I do regret the things I've left undone.' Major among these were occasions when he had not forgiven those who had wronged him. Now it was too late. In some cases those concerned had even predeceased him.

To forgive is something which we must never delay. You never know how soon it will be too late.

If the injured one could read your heart, you may be sure he would understand and pardon.

(Robert Louis Stevenson)

Unlocking a Door

SOMETIMES A door may be slammed shut in our face because of an unpleasant disagreement or falling out. This door, metaphorically, then seems to be permanently closed against us. Do not wait for it to be opened from the other side. You have the key to unlock it. You can do so with determination by showing a forgiving nature, one that is endowed with the capacity to forget an injury. The strongest lock will give way to these virtues, and those who are separated by that ugly door will meet again to renew a fulfilling companionship. Let no door stay closed for too long, as the lock might get rusty and then refuse to yield.

Good to forgive,
Better to forget.

(Robert Browning)

Mountaineering Over Molehills

IT HAS BEEN said, and has almost become a cliché, that it is not what you are eating that gives you ulcers but what is eating you. Often an innocent remark can be misinterpreted or exaggerated out of all proportion. Overly sensitive, a person can distort the remembrance of an actual event into a wild fantasy, and thus turn an innocuous statement into dynamite. Many a quarrel has been carried on over almost nothing, usually exacting a terrible price.

There are times when it might not be easy to overlook a slight, but it is clever. Defuse a volatile situation before it becomes a conflagration and beware of making mountains out of molehills.

We win by tenderness; we conquer by forgiveness.
(Frederick William Robertson)

Take the Initiative

NO MATTER WHOSE fault it is, do not wait for the other party to make the first attempt at reconciliation. It is even possible that they are only waiting for some indication on your part that you are ready to let bygones be bygones. Anger blinds us and we may not recognise the yearning for forgiveness that goes out to us from the other side. The other person may be reticent merely because they fear that you may reject their approach.

There is nothing more rewarding than for people who have become estranged to come together again, and replace the misery of ugly memories and the poison of resentment with the joy of 'making up'. What could be more beautiful than for you to take the initiative?

Oh, Great Father, never let me judge another man until I have walked in his moccasins for two weeks.

(Indian prayer)

A List of Steps to Reach Personal Forgiveness

THERE ARE A variety of ways in which to gain and give forgiveness. People differ in their temperament and there are thus numerous causes of conflict. To reach a reconciliation, we must choose the appropriate method, with the steps made to fit each individual case. However, there are some general rules we can follow.

✤ *Genuineness is a pre-condition of forgiveness.*

✤ *To be real and lasting, forgiveness needs working at and requires goodwill on both sides.*

If you are the offender:

✤ *Own up to the wrongs you have committed and ask for forgiveness, without reservation or cheap excuses.*

✤ *Never beg when apologising and seeking a reconciliation. Ask for forgiveness with dignity and deference to the other party.*

✤ *Follow your apology immediately and in every possible way by giving full restitution, and doing anything necessary to repair the damage done and to rectify the injustice committed.*

✤ *The wound inflicted may be deep and long-lasting and therefore might necessitate continued and repeated attempts at healing.*

✤ *Do not be discouraged. If first approaches are rejected or totally ignored, keep on trying. There might also be inevitable setbacks.*

✤ *Write a short note expressing your honest and profound regrets and your longing for reconciliation.*

❖ *Try to break down the wall of silence that may have built up between you by uttering the first word, perhaps by merely saying 'hello'.*

❖ *Lift the phone and try to meet, initially as it were, from a distance.*

❖ *Make use of every opportunity to establish renewed contact.*

❖ *Express your good wishes on an occasion of happiness. Send a 'get better' note in cases of sickness or an expression of sympathy when there is grief.*

❖ *Send a gift or card remembering a birthday, special anniversary or happy event, even if the other party conspicuously ignored one of yours.*

❖ *When accidentally meeting in the street, at a function or party, do not shun the other person. A mere nod might do to start with.*

❖ *Try to establish eye contact. A genuine smile may be responded to automatically before the other party realises they have done so. It will help in eventually breaking the ice.*

❖ *Once on talking terms, explain the circumstances that might have contributed to or actually caused the offence and the rift.*

If you have been offended:

❖ *Forgive unconditionally.*

❖ *Remember that to forgive is not a sign of weakness, but of strength. It does not diminish your stature but enhances it.*

❖ *Acknowledge notes or wishes you may receive, even by just two simple words like 'thank you'.*

❖ Try to make it easier for the offender by showing your readiness to forgive.

❖ Respond to their first tentative approaches.

❖ Encourage the offender in their efforts to make amends and realise how apprehensive they may be, fearing to be rebuffed by you.

❖ Consider that there might have been circumstances which, if not prompted, at least precipitated the offence.

❖ Remember that the wrongdoer is only human with all the weaknesses this implies. Perhaps they were burdened by problems and anxieties at the time, which made them not fully aware of the gravity of their offence.

❖ When extending the hand of forgiveness, do so humbly, without appearing patronising or in any way suggesting moral or ethical superiority. You only do what is right and which, in its ultimate effect, benefits both sides.

❖ Forgiveness must not be a mere smoothing over but a complete settlement.

Having reached the final stage of complete reconciliation is an exalting and joyous experience. You learn what forgiveness can do not only for you but to you. You have wiped the slate clean and all bad feelings are erased. Your lives, instead of being bitter, will become better.

Ways to Forgiveness

Three Magic Words

I T IS NOT belittling yourself or humiliating to say, 'I am
sorry'. Those three words act like a lubricant which
can make for a smooth relationship. Swallowing your
pride will never cause indigestion or loss of face.
However, the words must come from the heart and not
merely from the tongue.

**An angry man opens his mouth and closes
his mind.**

(Jewish Saying)

A Wise Rule of Life

WE ALL HAVE our faults and failings. Perfectionism may
be an ideal, but it is not a reality. Everyone is subject to
varying moods and the experience of upsetting incidents
that make us act differently from our real and usual
selves. It may be these very circumstances that cause
someone to offend and hurt you. Therefore, we must
learn to be tolerant. Instead of feeling anger, we should
go out of our way to remove the pain that may have led
the offender to cause trouble. This is a very constructive
way of forgiving.

You should forgive many things in others, but nothing in yourself.

(Ausonius)

Falling Out

MINOR DISAGREEMENTS about trivial matters which could easily and quickly have been settled are often exaggerated, eventually leading to a permanent estrangement. Trifling incidents, like a small oversight, a birthday forgotten or an unintentional slight, may break up even the closest links between people. A jealous outsider may even cunningly poison a precious relationship, their interference merely prompted by ill will and the desire to make mischief.

It is so easy to find fault, and wrongly accuse someone of neglect or of failing in their duty to give help at a time when it was most needed. If you know that the blame placed on you is unfounded and is based on a misunderstanding or on misinformation, do not stand aloof. Have it out. Do not feel cheapened by doing so, however much you are convinced that the fault is not yours and the reproach is unjustified. Should you find that the cause, without you suspecting it, was after all on your part, do not hold back in offering your apology and asking for forgiveness.

Either way it may take time to overcome feelings of ill will and rebuild the trust necessary to establishing a new relationship.

God forgives sins committed against him, but offences against man must first be forgiven by the injured person.

(Talmud)

Third Party Assistance

IF NEITHER SIDE succeeds in achieving a *rapprochement*, it shows not weakness but wisdom and concern to make use of a mediator. This may be a friend of both or someone known for their tact, ability and fairness in arbitration. Those belonging to a religious community will seek the aid of their minister.

Each night before retiring, forgive whomever offended you.

(Asher b. Yehiel)

Provisional Forgiveness

TWO LITTLE BROTHERS had a quarrel. Before going to bed their mother said to one of them, 'John, you must forgive James.' John was adamant that he would not. 'What happens if you die during the night? What will you say to God?', his mother persisted. 'Well, I'll forgive him,' the little boy now agreed, 'but if I don't die during the night, James better look out in the morning.'

This seems so childish an attitude, but do not many adults act the very same way? We are ready to forgive, temporarily, for the duration of a predicament or an emergency. Provisional forgiveness, however, is not true forgiveness. Forgiveness must be unconditional, final and absolute.

Who avenges subdues one, who forgives rules over two.

(I. Hurwitz)

An Unexpected Reaction

WITH VANDALISM abounding, it was nothing extraordinary when a young ruffian deliberately ran into an elderly woman carrying a basket of apples. He made her stumble and drop all her fruit.

Gleefully, the fellow then watched her distress and, adding insult to injury, stood by making fun of his unfortunate victim.

The woman ignored his jeers. Silently she picked up the apples one by one, and put them back into her basket. Having done so, she handed one of them to the dumbfounded youth saying, 'May God forgive you, just as I do'. It was something he had never expected. For the first time in his life, he felt a sense of shame. Instead of running away, as he would have done on any other occasion, he apologised to the woman. He said he was sorry and would never do it again, to anyone. Then, on the spur of the moment, he pulled some money out of his pocket, as an offering of reconciliation.

The woman refused to accept it. There was no need for it, she told him. To have made him realise his folly was plenty of restitution. The Bible says that 'a soft answer turns away anger' (Proverbs 15, 1). A pacifying reply can avoid much heartache. It is a simple but effective expression of forgiveness.

O God, forgive, I pray thee, those who have wronged me. . .

(Talmud)

The Noblest Revenge

A REBELLION HAD broken out in one district of a Chinese Emperor's realm. Mustering his forces, the Emperor marched against the rebels and soon routed them.

Everyone expected him to punish these enemies severely. To the surprise of all, however, he gave orders that the prisoners be treated with kindness. One of the generals remonstrated with the Emperor. The general reminded him of his previous determination to destroy the rebels who were his enemies. Instead he had pardoned them. 'Indeed, I destroyed my enemies,' the general was told. 'You see, I've made them my friends.'

The noblest revenge is to forgive.

(Thomas Fuller)

To Understand is to Forgive

WELL-KNOWN IS THE French proverb '*comprendre c'est pardonner*': that 'to understand is to forgive'. We might be lucky enough to have a smooth run in life or to be of a nature that can take disappointment and hardship with equanimity. Others may not be so fortunate. Adverse incidents or cares may weigh on their minds and make them edgy. They may do and say things they really do not mean. Accept their predicament. Do not take personally what was merely an emotional outburst, and was certainly not meant to hurt you. If you cannot ignore it, react by showing forgiveness and helping to alleviate the very cause that precipitated the 'offence'.

A woman met her friend in the street late one morning and could not help noticing her friend's agitation. Asked whether she was unwell, the friend replied that she was fine. However, she also admitted to being a little upset, as she explained, 'I've just had a telling off from my sister'.

She said that she frequently visited her sister, in case she could do some shopping for her. On that day, however, her sister had been out. Her sister's husband, who was at home, had promised to tell his wife that she had called and to say that she was sorry to have missed her. Somehow he forgot to give his wife this message. When, a few hours later, she called back, her sister, who meanwhile had returned, vehemently abused her, saying many unkind and bitter words. Worse still, her sister accused her of not thinking of her.

'And what did you say?', inquired the woman. 'Nothing!' her friend replied. 'I simply walked out. You see, my sister has lots of worries and I knew that her emotions had just run away with her.' 'I assume you won't visit your sister again?', the woman wondered. 'Far from it,' she said. 'Certainly, I will do so again. In fact, I'm going there now to take her some fruit.'

We forgive so long as we love.

(La Rochefoucauld)

Saying Yes to Yourself

A story from a sermon by the Reverend Terry Sweetser.

SOME YEARS AGO, a young man I know left home against his father's advice. The father, a wise but reserved man, was sure that his son was making a big mistake. The boy had decided to go to a seminary and become a minister. They had argued long and hard. The father pointed out all the drawbacks: too many bosses, too little money, too tenuous a job. The son countered by attacking. He accused his father of being disappointed that his son was not going to follow in his footsteps, and that he would not be satisfied unless his son became a professor, as he was.

Angry words were exchanged. They both dragged out the dirty linen of twenty years. The son was a spendthrift. The father was cheap. The son was flighty. The father was dull. The son was irresponsible.

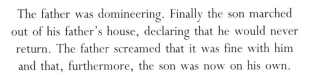

The father was domineering. Finally the son marched out of his father's house, declaring that he would never return. The father screamed that it was fine with him and that, furthermore, the son was now on his own.

The boy did go to a seminary. But some of his father's accusations were true and they haunted him. Not only did he feel insecure, but he also saw the practical results. The son was impulsive, so he soon ran short of money and commitment to his new venture. He could not pay his bills and was uninspired by his work. Good sense told him that he had to make some changes, but there seemed to be no meaning in it. He could not seem to believe in himself and began to flounder. He found some part-time work, but as his father had predicted, minimum-wage employment would not pay for going to school.

One morning when the boy awoke with a hangover and only a dollar to his name, he started replaying all his previous illusions. He fantasized about himself as a great preacher. He raged at the injustice of a life that allowed some people to have it easy while he struggled. Then he thought about his father living comfortably in the suburbs. At first he was resentful, but then he started to weep. He wished he could go home. He wished he could make peace.

He knew he could not go crawling back saying he had changed. His father would never believe it, and he knew he would never be able to live with it. Still, the boy realised he had grown and that he had been right about the ministry. He began to believe that if he could affirm the parts of himself that were good, even if they were different from his father's good points, he might be able to return. To really do well, he knew he would have to claim his past failures as well as his new consolation. He dressed and set out to see his father. On the way out the door he picked up his mail. In it he found a letter from his father. It contained a sizeable cheque and these words, 'I thought you might be running low. Much love, Dad.'

He went home. It was the first of many such returns. The two were very different and their differences would always grate on each other. As long as they both could find ways to accept themselves and each other's differences, though, return was always possible. Good sense told them it would be that way, but it always took a leap of faith to make the journey.

This story is a unique representation of the effect of forgiveness. In reality, it is not just a story. The Reverend Terry Sweetser added in his sermon that he was the boy and it had all happened to him. As a concluding thought to this story he reflected, 'What a wonderful thing would happen in this weary world if its prodigal people could take that leap of faith more often.'

The Finality of Forgiveness

AS FORGIVENESS must be absolute, it should be accepted as final. No good will ever come from any leftover conflict. Having rectified a wrong we have committed and obtained forgiveness, the issue should be considered closed.

Nevertheless, it may happen at times that a lingering sense of guilt continues to haunt us. Remorseful memories start intruding, creating an atmosphere of discontent and threatening our peace of mind. Nothing could be more damaging to all concerned.

Not 'letting go' has been compared to a car-horn that, having been sounded and served its purpose, gets stuck and keeps on blaring. To suffer from chronic self-reproach for a redundant reason helps no-one.

How could man live at all if he did not give absolution every night to himself and all his brothers?

(Goethe)

PROBLEMS OF FORGIVENESS

The Holes are Still There

ANY RECONCILIATION carries with it dangerous remnants of the wrong done, which we must learn to make ineffective. However completely we have forgiven, we cannot force ourselves to forget. These remnants can be compared with the scar that remains after one has undergone surgery. Even if the operation is a complete success, the scar is still there as a constant reminder. A story can be used to illustrate this fact of life. It recalls a practice one father had adopted to make his child realise that the effect of a wrong done can never be totally eliminated, even if one has gained forgiveness.

Each time the boy had done something causing pain or hurt, his father put a nail into the door of the child's room. The father promised however, that whenever the youngster performed an act of kindness or showed genuine regret for a misdemeanour, he would pull out one of the nails.

It became a challenge. Soon the number of nails grew ever less till one day not a single one remained. Proud of his achievement, the child excitedly called out, 'You see, Daddy, not one nail is left!'. 'That is true, my child,' replied the father, 'but the holes the nails made are still there.'

These holes are the indelible reminders left even after gaining and giving forgiveness. No matter how hard we try, we cannot obliterate them and the danger always exists that, against our own wishes, they make forgiveness incomplete. However, we can neutralise their effect by carrying no bitterness in our hearts, so that the 'holes' will belong to a dead past, and will be unable to influence our living present.

Forgiveness is perfect when the sin is not remembered.

(Arab Proverb)

A Misinterpreted Silence

A DIFFICULT SITUATION arises when we are ready to forgive but get no response from the person who has hurt us. After repeated abortive attempts on our part, we may just give up trying. Convinced that any further approach by us is futile we remain estranged and the conflict is unresolved.

We should consider the possibility that perhaps the person who has hurt us lacks the gift to say that they are sorry, and that hence their silence is not rejection. Give them the benefit of the doubt and, although you may regret their inability to respond, forgive them. Certainly, you will not be the loser.

I always seek the good that is in people and leave the bad to Him who made mankind and knows how to round off the corners.

(Goethe's mother)

A Chain Reaction

A MAN NEVER forgot a lesson he had been taught as a small boy. It happened in the depth of winter. Early one morning when he was looking out of his bedroom window which faced on to the farmyard, he watched the cows, sheep and horses patiently waiting to be hand-fed. As there was little room for them to move, the animals were packed tightly together. They just stood there, placidly expecting their fodder.

Suddenly one cow tried to turn around. In the attempt, she pushed hard against the animal standing next to her which immediately reacted by kicking a neighbouring animal. Within no time at all, a serene scene had changed into one of turmoil with the animals shoving, kicking and butting each other.

When telling his mother what he had seen, she took the opportunity to apply his observation to life generally. 'Always remember,' she told him, 'how the fight in the yard started and the consequences of giving as good as you get.' It takes wisdom and strength of character to take a knock without retaliating. Otherwise you might trigger off a chain reaction, with the results being far worse than the initial minor harm.

Nothing is more costly, nothing is more sterile, than vengeance.

(Winston Churchill)

Vested Interests

THERE ARE WRONG motives for showing (or asking for) forgiveness. Those who seek or give it for selfish reasons deceive themselves. Their forgiveness is not real and will not last. Forgiveness is made into a sham if it is practiced to gain a personal advantage because the other party is influential or powerful. Equally fallacious and ineffectual is the pursuit of forgiveness if it is prompted by fear, whether of social ostracism or Divine punishment.

The practice of always 'smoothing things over' also shows mere self-interest. Other wrong motives for desiring reconciliation include missing a broken friendship, wanting to restore a lost business connection or no longer being able to take part in activities one used to enjoy. Beware most of those who say, 'I forgive you because I am good.' Forgiveness must be sought after for its own sake, in the realisation of its innate value.

Without forgiveness life is governed by . . . an endless cycle of resentment and retaliation.

(Robert Assagioli)

Excuses

EXCUSES MUST NOT be used as reasons for forgiving. How often does one hear that 'it wasn't my fault' or 'I just couldn't help it'? This is just 'buck-passing': trying to blame everyone else instead of taking the responsibility on yourself, which takes a lot of courage. Some things cannot be brushed aside or depicted as too insignificant.

Excuses do not let the offender off and some wrongs are tolerable only once. Some people commit wrongs which may go beyond the normal forgiveness boundaries, and therefore forgiving them does not lessen or condone the evil that they have done. One cannot change the past by forgiving, only the hurt that came from it.

To use the excuse that one is a victim of circumstances or that one's wrong-doing is the result of feelings of insecurity is wrong. Neither excuse is a reason to hurt others.

Since I myself stand in need of God's pity, I have granted an amnesty to all my enemies.

(Heinrich Heine)

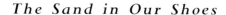

The Sand in Our Shoes

AN ADVENTUROUS HIKER had set out to traverse some very difficult terrain. Numerous obstacles obstructed his way. He had to climb steep mountains and cross deep gullies, and the journey was made even more arduous by the burning sun and the pouring rain.

Undaunted, however, he kept going. He managed to surmount all these hazards and to reach his destination. When he was recalling his experiences, he disclosed that the only thing which almost defeated him was sand in his shoes!

All through life, it seems, it is frequently not the large issues that get us down and cause offence, but the insignificant, even petty occurrences. They threaten to open up chasms between ourselves and our fellow human beings. They come in all forms: a minor unpleasantness which we cannot dismiss from our mind; an argument about a truly trifling matter, now blown out of all proportion; or a small unfairness now magnified into an intolerable injustice.

Learn to ignore meaningless slights and annoyances which, inevitably, come everyone's way. Show that you are above them. Keep the right perspective and a sense of proportion worthy of an intelligent human being. Ignore the puny gnawing things of life, recognising their pettiness and yet possible danger. In short, empty out the grains of sand from your shoes.

We win by tenderness, we conquer by forgiveness.

(Frederick William Robertson)

Of a Quarrelsome Nature

SOME PEOPLE ARE innately quarrelsome. Sooner or later, they will fall out with everybody, including those closest to them. For no reason they pick fights. Never admitting that it is they themselves who have caused the rift, they will always blame others.

It does not take long for these people to lose the few friends who may have stood by them. Ultimately avoided by all, they become lonely individuals, eaten up by jealousy and resentment. All the more, they continue to act in ways calculated to upset and annoy. They will do so out of spite or revenge for an imagined wrong that they have suffered.

If you have been the victim of such malevolence and have failed in all your attempts of a *rapprochement*, you may regard it as futile to make any further efforts. In fact, you may find that even if you were able to achieve what appeared to be a reconciliation, there would be a quick recurrence of all that had happened previously. It is so easy to then wash your hands and leave such a person to their own devices. Remember, however, that in spite of everything, they are in need of help. Carry no grudge but forgive them for what they cannot help doing.

Only the brave know how to forgive, it is the most refined and generous pitch of virtue that human nature can arrive at.

(Laurence Sterne)

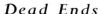

Dead Ends

WELL AWARE OF the importance of vision, Leonardo da Vinci divided society into three categories. There are those who see unaided, those who see when they are shown, and those who cannot see at all.

Fortunate indeed are those who easily grasp a situation. Well worthwhile is the effort to help those of the second category, in order to make them recognise the circumstances responsible for hurt and havoc. Those who belong to the third category should not be blamed for their inability to respond. They seem to be at a dead end, and their need for help is thus paramount. Typical of this latter group are those who cannot see (and therefore cannot ever consider) any possibility of reconciliation. They are convinced that the harm done to them is 'unforgivable' and the damage caused is irreparable. They will reject any approach on the part of the offender as meaningless and insincere.

Do not give in to their refusal to respond. Do not give up, and spare no effort to make them realise that no offence is unforgivable unless one makes it so.

An unforgiving mind has its own agenda. It includes distorting what is real until it is barely recognisable.

(G. Jampolsky)

A Practical Guide on the Way to Collective Forgiveness

OF SUPREME IMPORTANCE is the achievement of reconciliation between races and nations, to heal the wounds left by wars and wrongs done. Like the search for forgiveness among individuals, a single attempt is inadequate. It demands a succession and, possibly, a multiplicity of endeavours which, combined, will finally reach their goal.

Some of the steps suggested below may be pursued simultaneously, though it might be necessary, with others, to follow a certain sequence, which is implied in the way they are listed here. These suggestions have been adopted from examples which have already proved successful in various parts of the world.

❖ *It is necessary to reach full recognition and admission of the wrongs done.*

❖ *One must show an expression of genuine regret and a sense of shame.*

❖ *It is necessary to ask for forgiveness.*

❖ *In a case of law, it is necessary to reach a just punishment of the instigators and perpetrators of the crimes which is determined by an independent court of judges; the sentences must be arrived at with mercy and are not to be tainted by thoughts of revenge.*

❖ *There must be a determination to repair the damage done to the very maximum of possibility and with the promise of a full restitution and restoration.*

❖ *If necessary, there should be repeated face-to-face meetings between the parties concerned, where everyone can openly discuss past misdeeds and explore the various ways to achieve reconciliation and forgiveness.*

❖ *There must be initiation of an ongoing dialogue.*

❖ *The parties concerned must apply every means possible to foster a new spirit of constructive cooperation, doing things together to generate a sense of community that will replace all alienation.*

❖ *Those involved could become sharers in projects especially chosen to give a helping hand to some jointly decided upon deserving cause.*

❖ *One must put former grievances and antagonisms permanently to rest.*

❖ *The people affected could hold sporting events and competitions. It was particularly to create bonds of friendship between former enemies that, in 1896, after an interval of 1,502 years, Baron Pierre de Coubertin revived the Olympic Games. Metaphorically speaking, the playing field was meant to replace the battlefield.*

❖ *Notable indeed is the power of music as a means to calm ruffled passions and to inspire a happy and friendly spirit. Music can be used to replace the discord of dissonance by the harmony of unity. In the words of Horace, music is a 'healing balm of troubles'.*

❖ *Finally, upon reaching the stage of forgiveness, those concerned could celebrate jointly, to create a sense of joy and peace. Not least, this celebration should engender a combined effort to contribute to the prevention of any recurrence of the evils perpetrated.*

RELIGION AND FORGIVENESS

Divine Forgiveness

A SAGE WAS asked whether God would forgive an offender who showed genuine regret. The wise man countered the question with another one. 'Do you throw away your overcoat if it has a tear in it?' 'Certainly not,' was the reply, 'I repair it'. 'If you are so careful with your belongings,' the sage now remarked, 'don't you expect God to look after his children likewise?'

Those believing in a God who is perfect love are confident that even the worst of malefactors can hope for his ultimate forgiveness. In fact, God is anxiously waiting for their return, however long delayed.

The German poet Heinrich Heine rather cynically observed that for all his misdemeanours he personally could still count on God's forgiveness because 'the good God will forgive me, that's his business'. There is a significant proviso to this. The offender must acknowledge the wrong they have done and the unhappiness they have caused, and then make full restitution for their actions.

No man who will not forgive his neighbour can believe that God is willing, yea wanting to forgive him.

(George MacDonald)

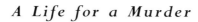

A Life for a Murder

NOTHING CAN SURPASS acts of kindness and forgiveness
performed in the midst of ugly hatred and horrendous
bloodshed. In one of the many gruesome conflicts
that have raged between different races, people
and ethnic groups, a girl had witnessed a blood-thirsty
soldier pursuing her brother and cruelly killing him.
She would have suffered the same fate had she not
managed to escape.

Some time later, with the fighting still in progress, a
badly wounded soldier was brought into the hospital
in which the girl worked as a nurse. She identified
him at once as the killer of her brother, his features
having been indelibly printed on her mind.
Now he needed constant nursing to survive.
She gave it to him unstintingly.

On his recovery, when being told who the nurse was to
whom he owed his life, he insisted on seeing her. He
wanted to ask her why she had done so. Had it not been
her opportunity to avenge her brother's death? She had
saved his life, she said, 'because my religion teaches me to
forgive those who are my enemies and try to harm me'.

To be able to forget and forgive is the
prerogative of a noble soul.

(Stekel, Autobiography)

Unjustified Blame

A MOTHER WAS dying of cancer. A deeply pious woman,
she would never question God's ways. Nor was she
hypocritical. Even so, it was beyond her young
daughter's comprehension when she one day overheard
her mother, who was suffering great agonies of pain,
mutter, 'I thank God'. Taken aback, the daughter asked
her mother how she could thank God in the face of
all her affliction. She never forgot her mother's reply.
'My child, you must thank God for the good and
for the bad.'

With all the phenomenal advances of our knowledge, we
have merely extended the horizons of our ignorance.
The more we learn, the less we understand. To blame
God for afflictions and miseries would assign to us a
power of comprehension we do not possess. How do we
know that pain or disasters are of God's making? If we
have no reason to hold God responsible, we cannot
blame him nor does he need forgiveness. Indeed, for the
religiously-minded, the time of affliction is the very
moment to ask for God's help and support.

His heart was as great as the world but there
was no room in it to hold the memory of a wrong.

(Ralph Waldo Emerson)

Can God Be Forgiven?

THE HARDEST question of all, for those adhering to a faith, is trying to explain the suffering of the innocent. How can a God who is all-powerful and benevolent permit the pain, sickness, agony and tragedy that happens to so many good people? Can we ever forgive him for it?

One partial answer to this question that has been given by theologians throughout the ages, refers to God's most precious gift to humans — free will. Without it we would be mere puppets and automatons. Therefore, there is no need to forgive God, as he cannot be blamed for human suffering. So much misfortune in the world is only too obviously a result of people abusing their free will.

This answer however, is not completely satisfactory. Job, the righteous and good man of the Bible whose very name has become synonymous with the innocent sufferer, refused to curse God and did so for a different reason. His deep faith convinced him that 'my Redeemer lives'. Even the evil that befalls us must have a purpose.

We must forgive God because of our lack of understanding. Our mind just cannot penetrate some of the vast mysteries of the universe or grapple with its fundamental enigmas, not least of which is the suffering of the innocent. One day, perhaps, we may find a meaningful explanation which will become one of the many pieces that make up the mosaic of life.

Forgiving God is of no benefit to him, only to
the forgiver. Harold S. Kushner, in his widely-read book
When Bad Things Happen to Good People (Pan Books Ltd,
London 1982), exonerates God from any responsibility
for life's tragedies and thereby from any need of
forgiveness. You cannot blame God for the suffering of
the innocent, according to Kushner's view which
deviates from that of traditional monotheist religions,
because it happened in a reality independent of his will
and closed to his interference. In fact, God, in his
compassion and love, shares the suffering and anguish of
those stricken, standing by them and helping them to
bear their burden.

*What? shall we receive good at the hand of God,
and shall we not receive evil?*

(Job 2, 10)

Applied Religion

ALL RELIGIONS have taught forgiveness. Unequivocally,
they demand of their followers not to take vengeance or
to bear grudges, but to forgive even one's enemies and,
going to the extreme, to turn the other cheek.
Nevertheless, many wrongs have been committed in the
name of religion. Far from forgiving evil done, acts of
revenge have shown so-called (and self-styled) 'religious'
persons and communities to be instead consumed by
hatred and vengefulness. They have been conspicuous by
their practice of not forgiving.

This has been the reason for religion to be condemned altogether by some. However, individual cases of wrongs done in the name of a deity must not be generalised. Fanaticism blinds the eye. It will sanction and rationalise anything done on its behalf. It provides no justification for the claim that these actions and lack of forgiveness prove the failure of religion altogether. To do so would be a misconception.

At the famous 'Speakers' Corner' in London's Hyde Park, a man standing on his box was holding forth on religion and all the good that it promised. He sounded like a real crank and was being constantly heckled by the crowd that had gathered around him. One of the listeners taunting him shouted out, 'Religion has been on this earth for thousands of years and look at the state of the world!'. Without a moment's hesitation the speaker retorted, 'Water has been on this earth for millions of years and look at your dirty face!'.

Religion has not failed, but people have failed to apply its teachings, especially that of forgiveness.

He who forgiveth and is reconciled unto his enemy, shall receive his reward from God.

(Koran, Sura 'Counsel', XLII, 38)

LEGENDS
AND ANECDOTES
OF FORGIVENESS

Though the significance of forgiveness has been
recognised universally among all cultures and races,
it is regrettably not often practised. However, in a
colourful variety of ways various cultures have
highlighted its paramount importance, particularly in
these legends and anecdotes.

Forgiveness Worth Emulating

When he was president of the United States
(1897–1901), William McKinley was specially beloved
for his conciliatory nature. In spite of this, it was
inevitable that, like most people in public office, he had
to experience abuse at times. This occurred most often
during political campaigns.

On one such campaign during winter, a determined
young reporter, employed by a paper run by the opposite
political party, tailed McKinley wherever he went. The
reporter made use of every opportunity to misrepresent
McKinley's views and to hold him up to ridicule. Instead
of resenting him, McKinley respected the reporter's very
persistence. After all, was he not trying his utmost to
fulfil the assignment he had been given?

When the temperature dropped to freezing point, McKinley's admiration turned into pity. Travelling to his next destination in an enclosed carriage, he was well fortified against the cold. However, he noticed that the reporter, sitting next to the driver outside and not prepared for the harsh weather, was exposed to the biting cold and was shivering badly. Stopping the coach, McKinley asked the reporter to come and join him inside the carriage. He even placed his own coat around the reporter's shoulders. The reporter was convinced that McKinley could not have realised who he was and what he had been doing during the campaign. Identifying himself, he added that the president should make no mistake and that, in spite of his concern, 'I shall continue to defame you.' Smiling, McKinley assured him that he was well-informed of it all. 'But I bear you no grudge. Just as I am trying to do my duty, so are you. I've specially asked you to join me in the warmth of this carriage so that you can do your job properly!'

Whenever we encounter disparagement, it is well worth emulating McKinley's type of forgiveness. Wishing well even those who want to harm us shows nobility of spirit.

Force may subdue, but love gains; and he that forgives first, wins the laurels.

(William Penn)

A Pupil of Liszt

TO GAIN RECOGNITION, a young pianist going on tour had advertised herself as 'a pupil of Franz Liszt', which she was not. One day when she was about to give a recital in a small town, once again doing so under the false claim, it so happened that Liszt was visiting this very place as well. There was every likelihood that her deception would be exposed, cutting short her career.

There was only one thing for her to do. She called on Liszt, confessing how she had abused his name. Her excuse was that she depended on her recitals to make a living, and that by claiming to be his pupil, she was sure to attract an audience. Genuinely sorry, she asked the great piano virtuoso to forgive her. Liszt did not fail to express his displeasure at her wrongful use of his name and stated that he could not approve of her ruse.

Nevertheless, he was a man of forgiveness and showed it in his own unique way. He asked the girl to sit down and play for him. Listening to her, he had to correct her technique on a few occasions. There was no doubt in his mind, however, that the girl possessed talent. When she had finished the piece and was about to leave, still afraid of the composer's anger, he gave her the most wonderful surprise — forgiveness in the form of a gift. 'I've now taught you something and from now on you are entitled to call yourself "a pupil of Liszt" ', he said.

One who is begged for forgiveness should not be so cruel as not to forgive.

(Rashi)

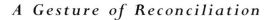

A Gesture of Reconciliation

ONE DAY, Charles Dickens and Douglas Jerrold, who had been close friends for many years, had a disagreement. It made them stop speaking to each other.

Weeks later, they accidentally met in a café. They acted like strangers. Purposely they sat down with their backs to each other. But not for long. Suddenly Jerrold turned round and, facing his one-time friend, spoke to him. 'Charles,' he said, 'for heaven's sake, shake hands. Life is too short for this.' Greatly relieved, Dickens instantly grasped his hand, saying that if Jerrold had not spoken first, he would have done so.

People will sometimes forgive you the good you have done them, but seldom the harm they have done you.

(Somerset Maughan)

For the Young

ORGIVENESS SHOULD BE practised from our earliest days. It is therefore extremely important to make our children realise its significance. First of all, our own lifestyle should serve as an example. What happens at home is absorbed by the young and instinctively copied by them. However, we must not neglect to guide them as well, both at home and at school, by pointing out to them the multiple aspects and many ways of forgiveness. The following legend, which is really meant for all who are young in heart, may be of help in this endeavour.

King Solomon and the Little Bee

LEGEND TELLS THAT King Solomon, renowned for his wisdom, was even able to speak the language of animals. At the beginning of every year, the beasts of the fields and forests, as well as the birds and insects of the air, came to his palace to pay their respects and express their good wishes to the king.

On one such occasion, the palace was once again packed with every type of creature. Among them was a little bee, sitting with her parents in the section reserved for insects. Seeing the mighty ruler for the very first time, she admired his handsome looks. Particularly attracted by his nose, she suddenly felt the urge to sting it. Making a 'beeline' to Solomon's face, she stung him on his left nostril. This, of course, hurt the king and he became very angry. However, when the little bee apologised, saying how sorry she was and promising never to do it again, King Solomon forgave her. Happily she flew back to her parents.

Three weeks after this incident, the Queen of Sheba was visiting the king. Bowing before Solomon's throne, she told him that she was about to test his wisdom. 'I am going to ask you three questions,' she said. 'Should you fail to answer even one of them, I shall tell the whole world that I, the Queen of Sheba, surpass you in wisdom!' When Solomon consented to this test, she immediately put forward her first question. 'What is the most valuable possession anyone can have?', she asked. Not hesitating for a moment, the king replied that it was wisdom. More precious than rubies, its value exceeded that of even the finest gold. The queen could only agree. Money and property are never secure. However, no-one can take from us what we have learnt — the wealth gathered in our minds.

The second riddle concerned the best kind of meal. Once again, the king was in no doubt. 'Better by far is a meal of the simplest food, when prepared with love, than the most sumptuous feast served in an atmosphere of unfriendliness.' With two questions answered to her satisfaction, the queen now clapped her hands. Two men entered the room, each holding what appeared to be a beautiful rose. 'One of these flowers is real,' the queen informed the king, 'whilst the other one is artificial. Can you, without touching or smelling the roses, point out

to me the real one?'. The flowers appeared identical in
every respect and, after a careful and prolonged study of
the two specimens, the king was still at a loss as to
which was the real rose. He was about to concede his
ignorance when a little bee came buzzing through the
open window. Settling on the real rose, the bee began
to sip its nectar. There was no longer any doubt in the
king's mind as to which of the two flowers was the
natural one.

The Queen of Sheba was now convinced that Solomon
was indeed the wisest of humans. After her departure,
the king called the little bee to thank her. It was the
very bee that had stung his nose and had roused his
anger not so long ago. 'Please don't thank me,' she said.
'You may remember that after I had stung your nose, I
told you how sorry I was. But I also know that it is not
enough merely to say so. The proper way to show
regret is to make amends by doing something good for
the person one has hurt.'

To redress any wrong we have done, it is necessary to
follow three stages. Firstly, we must have the courage to
admit our mistake and the honesty to apologise. Then
we must resolve never to let it happen again.
Thirdly, and most of all, we must make up for it by
showing extra kindness and consideration to whomever
we have hurt.

EPILOGUE

Having the Last Word

HAVING RESOLVED A disagreement, it is essential that the expression of forgiveness is unambiguous and lasting. It must never carry even the suspicion of a compromise or a temporary solution.

Some people may unintentionally undo all the good that forgiveness has achieved by trying to have the last word relating to the conflict. However, in doing so they not only leave a bitter taste behind, but plant a time-bomb of tension that renders all forgiveness tenuous.

If you want to have the last word, let it express genuine happiness at having reached a reconciliation.

He who forgives ends the quarrel.

(African Proverb)

From a prayer by Robert Louis Stevenson.

Lord, enlighten us to see the beam that is in our own eye,
and blind us to the mote that is in our brother's.
Let us feel our offences. . . make them great and bright
before us. . . Blind us to the offences of our beloved,
cleanse them from our memories, take them out of our
mouths for ever.

Angus&Robertson

An imprint of HarperCollins *Publishers*, Australia

First published in Australia in 1995
Copyright © R. Brasch

HarperCollins*Publishers*
25 Ryde Road, Pymble, Sydney NSW 2073, Australia
31 View Road, Glenfield, Auckland 10, New Zealand
77–85 Fulham Palace Road, London W6 8JB, United Kingdom
Hazelton Lanes, 55 Avenue Road, Suite 2900,
Toronto, Ontario, M5R 3L2
and 1995 Markham Road, Scarborough, Ontario, M1B 5M8, Canada
10 East 53rd Street, New York NY 10032, United States of America

National Library of Australia Cataloguing-in-Publication data:

Brasch, R. (Rudolph), 1912–
A book of forgiveness.
ISBN 0 207 18803 3.
1. Forgiveness. I. Title.
179.9

Illustrated by Christie Cooper
Printed in Hong Kong

9 8 7 6 5 4 3 2 1
99 98 97 96 95